What's Done in the Dark Will Come to Light

A Lesson in Integrity

Shawntel D. Carey

SDC Compass Publishing LLC

What's Done in the Dark Will Come to Light

A Lesson in Integrity

SDC Compass Publishing LLC

sdccompasspublishingllc@gmail.com

Scripture quotations are taken from the
King James Version (KJV) of the Bible.

Cover and Interior Design by Shawntel D. Carey

Printed in the United States of America

Library of Congress Control Number: 2026939729

ISBN: 979-8-9939033-5-4

DEDICATION

Dedicated to those seeking a personal relationship with God. May this book strengthen your commitment to walking in integrity, ensuring your inner faith matches your outward actions even when no one is watching.

INTRODUCTION

The following saying has been passed down through generations:

"What is done in the dark will come to light."

Though simple, this truth carries weight far beyond culture or tradition. It reflects a moral reality recognized throughout history and affirmed in biblical teaching. While individuals may conceal things from one another, nothing is hidden from God. Scripture makes this clear: what is concealed will be revealed, and what is hidden will be made known.

This book is both a reminder and an invitation to choose integrity.

Integrity is not only about avoiding wrongdoing. It is about alignment, discipline, and living the truth so that who we are in private is the same as who we are in public.

INTRODUCTION

Alignment with God's Word requires consistency between inner faith and outward actions, demonstrated through a steadfast commitment to integrity, even under temptation, pressure, or when no one is watching.

This book's journey moves through a clear progression: truth leads to exposure, integrity calls for alignment, darkness carries consequence, light brings transformation, practice requires discipline, and grace offers redemption.

Choose to follow God's Word and walk in the light.

To live with integrity is to live freely.

TABLE OF CONTENTS

Chapter One

Truth Revealed

Truth Revealed

The phrase "what is done in the dark will come to light" reflects a principle found repeatedly in Scripture, particularly in the King James Version (KJV) of the Bible.

Luke 8:17 states:
"For nothing is secret, that shall not be made manifest; neither any thing hid, that shall not be known and come abroad."

Ecclesiastes 12:14 reiterates:
"For God shall bring every work into judgment, with every secret thing, whether it be good, or whether it be evil."

Throughout Scripture, this foundational concept is clear: hidden actions will eventually be revealed. The consequences of lacking integrity often lead to internal psychological turmoil.

Reflection

King David's sin with Bathsheba was concealed for a time, yet it was eventually exposed. Judas betrayed Jesus quietly, yet his actions became known. (2 Samuel 11–12; Matthew 26:14-16, KJV)

These accounts remind us that deception may survive for a season, but truth will ultimately be revealed.

This is not merely a religious concept. It is a predictable pattern of moral and ethical failure observable in everyday life.

Secrets are harmful. Deception multiplies confusion, leading to conflict and misunderstandings. Falsehoods result in a loss of credibility, producing guilt, shame, and diminished self-respect.

Truth requires no defense.

In time, whatever is hidden will be revealed.

Suggested Reading

Specific KJV Passages for Chapter One:

Luke 12:2-3

"For there is nothing covered, that shall not be revealed; neither hid, that shall not be known. Therefore whatsoever ye have spoken in darkness shall be heard in the light; and that which ye have spoken in the ear in closets shall be proclaimed upon the housetops."

Luke 8:17

"For nothing is secret, that shall not be made manifest; neither any thing hid, that shall not be known and come abroad."

Mark 4:22

"For there is nothing hidden, which shall not be manifested; neither was any thing kept secret, but that it should come abroad."

Ecclesiastes 12:14

"For God shall bring every work into judgment, with every secret thing, whether it be good, or whether it be evil."

Prayer

Heavenly Father,

You see everything; You know me through and through, every detail of my life.

Help me live authentically before You, upholding Your word and believing in the unseen.

Empower me to walk with integrity daily, letting my actions reflect Your light.

In Jesus name, I pray

Amen.

Chapter Two

Understanding Integrity

Understanding Integrity

Honesty is telling the truth. Integrity is living the truth.

Integrity means doing what is right even when no one is watching. It means that a person's private character matches their public persona. When integrity is present, there is consistency and alignment between values, words, and actions.

Proverbs 10:9 (KJV) states:
"He that walketh uprightly walketh surely:
but he that perverteth his ways shall be known."

This verse offers a clear warning: dishonesty may provide short-term advantages, but integrity is the only path to true and lasting security. A person who lives with integrity, honesty, and moral consistency lives with confidence; having nothing to hide and no reason to fear exposure. In contrast, a person who engages in dishonest or crooked behavior will eventually be exposed. Deceit cannot remain hidden; true character will inevitably come to light.

Reflection

Reputation is what people say about you but character is what God knows about you. Integrity is the decision to value character over reputation. A person with integrity does not rely on appearances or external approval. Integrity creates stability. It removes the need to manage falsehoods or maintain hidden versions of oneself. When integrity guides decisions, the fear of exposure disappears because there is nothing to hide.

The foundation of integrity produces:

- Internal harmony and mental clarity

- Deep, resilient trust, which is the foundation of meaningful relationships

- Reliability and dependability both personally and professionally

- Reduced conflict through transparency and honesty; avoiding resentment and misunderstandings

- Moral courage; a consistent commitment to doing what is right

Reflection

A person of integrity develops resilience in times of crisis. When principles are firmly established, there is no need to deliberate over ethical decisions; the course of action is already clear.

A life committed to integrity builds a lasting legacy of character. People remember not only what was achieved, but the consistent and honorable way in which it was achieved.

Suggested Reading

Specific KJV Passages for Chapter Two:

Proverbs 11:3

"The integrity of the upright shall guide them: but the perverseness of transgressors shall destroy them."

Proverbs 28:18

"Whoso walketh uprightly shall be saved: but he that is perverse in his ways shall fall at once."

Proverbs 20:7

"The just man walketh in his integrity: his children are blessed after him."

Psalm 25:21

"Let integrity and uprightness preserve me; for I wait on thee."

Psalm 101:2

"I will behave myself wisely in a perfect way. O when wilt thou come unto me? I will walk within my house with a perfect heart."

The following provides options for deeper study and key figures that lived with integrity.

Understanding integrity in Scripture involves studying uprightness, honesty, and consistent character. These passages emphasize that integrity provides guidance, stability, and protection.

For deeper study, consider:

- The book of Proverbs for daily wisdom on upright living
- Psalm 101 as a personal commitment to integrity
- 1 Samuel 12 as an example of leadership grounded in honesty

Key Examples:

- **Book of Job**
  Job retained his integrity despite losing everything
- **1 Samuel**
  Samuel maintained honesty and did not misuse his position
- **Book of Genesis**
  Joseph resisted temptation through moral conviction
- **Book of Daniel**
  Daniel earned trust because he was free from corruption

Prayer

Heavenly Father,

Grant me the strength to act with righteousness. As You look upon my heart, mold it to reflect Your likeness.

Teach me to value integrity and to guard my character above all outward appearances. Shape me to reflect Your truth in my every action.

Empower me to choose righteousness when no one is watching, and to seek Your guidance above all.

In Jesus name, I pray.

Amen.

Chapter Three

Cost of Living in Darkness

Cost of Living in Darkness

In biblical teaching, "living in darkness" is a metaphor for a life separated from God, characterized by sin, spiritual ignorance, and moral confusion. It is not only a moral failure, it is a path that leads to spiritual ruin, broken fellowship with God, and eventual and inevitable exposure to darkness.

God is defined as "light" (1 John 1:5, KJV):

"This then is the message which we have heard of him, and declare unto you, that God is light, and in him is no darkness at all."

Darkness, therefore, is the absence of His presence, guidance and truth. It represents a life lived without divine direction, often resulting in a life of deception, wickedness, and ultimately, spiritual death.

The relationship between dishonesty and darkness is clear. Dishonesty may offer temporary benefit, but the cost of living in darkness is the continual absence of God and the truth. Yet the cost of living in darkness is the habitual absence of the grace of God, leading to the loss of one's soul, divine favor, and peace, and ultimately to destruction.

Truth may feel difficult in the moment,
but the burden of deception demands a far greater cost.

Reflection

Reflective aspects of darkness and the cost in Scripture:

Separation from God

Light represents the presence of God, while darkness reflects a state of estrangement from the Creator. This separation leads to living according to self-centered desires rather than by the wisdom of God. (Psalm 101:7, KJV)

Sin and Moral Resistance

Preferring evil rather than light is not due to a lack of knowledge, but an immoral choice to blindly live in darkness. A person's actions cannot withstand the scrutiny of God's truth. A sinner is driven by the desire to conceal evil deeds because it offers a hiding place for their wrongdoings. (John 3:19–20, KJV)

Reflection

Spiritual Ignorance

A lack of spiritual understanding is equivalent to a state of darkness. It is a condition of being blinded, where one does not know where they are going because they have rejected or have yet to receive the Light of God. Those living in dishonesty often resist the light because they fear exposure. This creates a life driven by fear, guilt, and the continual need to conceal "the hidden things of dishonesty."
(1 John 2:11; 2 Corinthians 4:2, KJV)

The Realm of Evil

Darkness stands in direct opposition to the Kingdom of God, which is the kingdom of light. Scripture associates darkness with the dominion of Satan and spiritual forces of evil. (Ephesians 6:12, KJV)

Reflection

Trial of Darkness

Scripture also presents a different form of darkness. A faithful person may "walk in darkness" and have "no light." In this context, darkness is not a sign of sin, but a season of trial, grief, or silence from God. Even in this state, the believer is encouraged to remain steadfast in their faith, trusting in Him, despite the absence of clarity. (Isaiah 50:10, KJV)

The Nature of Lying

Jesus identifies the nature of deceit as originating entirely from the evil, stating that the devil is a liar and the father of lies. Dishonesty may offer immediate, "sweet" rewards, but its end is destructive: temporary gain, lasting ruin. A dishonest life creates a barrier between the individual and God, who is light. It also breaks trust within one's community, damaging credibility and leaving a reputation difficult to restore without repentance through God and faith in our Lord Jesus Christ. The ultimate cost of persistent, unrepentant dishonesty is severe, extending beyond this life into final judgment. (John 8:44; Psalm 101:7; Revelation 21:8, KJV)

Suggested Reading

Specific KJV Passages for Chapter Three:

Proverbs 20:17
"Bread of deceit is sweet to a man; but afterwards his mouth shall be filled with gravel.”

Proverbs 13:11
"Wealth gotten by vanity shall be diminished: but he that gathereth by labour shall increase."

Psalm 101:7
"He that worketh deceit shall not dwell within my house: he that telleth lies shall not tarry in my sight."

2 Corinthians 4:2
"But have renounced the hidden things of dishonesty, not walking in craftiness, nor handling the word of God deceitfully; but by manifestation of the truth commending ourselves to every man's conscience in the sight of God.”

Revelation 21:8

"But the fearful, and unbelieving, and the abominable, and murderers, and whoremongers, and sorcerers, and idolaters, and all liars, shall have their part in the lake which burneth with fire and brimstone: which is the second death"

Numbers 32:23

"But if ye will not do so, behold, ye have sinned against the Lord: and be sure your sin will find you out."

Galatians 6:7

"Be not deceived; God is not mocked: for whatsoever a man soweth, that shall he also reap."

Proverbs 28:13

"He that covereth his sins shall not prosper: but whoso confesseth and forsaketh them shall have mercy."

Luke 16:10

"He that is faithful in that which is least is faithful also in much: and he that is unjust in the least is unjust also in much."

Prayer

Lord Jesus,

I pray for my soul and for all who are lost in darkness.

Father God, You are the ultimate source of light and truth.

Grant me spiritual insight, a deeper connection with You, and the ability to discern Your will.

Protect my heart from lies, deception, and wrongdoing.

In the name of Jesus, I pray

Amen.

Chapter Four

Walking in the Light

Walking in the Light

The good news is that practicing integrity offers an alternative path to living in darkness. The Bible encourages believers to walk openly in the light. Scripturally, walking in the light signifies living in truth, holiness, and fellowship with God.

1 John 1:7 (KJV) states:
"But if we walk in the light, as he is in the light, we have fellowship one with another, and the blood of Jesus Christ his Son cleanseth us from all sin."

Our Lord Jesus Christ, the Light, brings transformation, purity, and spiritual understanding. A person who walks in the light does not fear exposure, because their life is not built on concealment.

Integrity brings peace of mind. It strengthens relationships and builds trust with others. When people know that your words can be trusted, your influence grows naturally.

The light removes fear and replaces anxiety with confidence. Living openly may require courage, but it produces peace and freedom. This is not simply a change in what we see, but a transformation in who we are; believers are "light in the Lord."

Reflection

Walking in the Light according to Scripture

Fellowship and Continual Cleansing

Walking in the light means living honestly before God. It is not a call to perfection, but to authenticity, bringing struggles into the open rather than concealing them. Fellowship becomes possible in the light, creating genuine community among believers. The cleansing described in Scripture is continual; as we remain in the light, the blood of Jesus Christ purifies us from sin. (1 John 1:7, KJV)

Identity and Morality

Walking in the light reflects a transformed life. It is a daily pattern of belief and obedience to the Lord. The fruit of the light, or the fruit of the Spirit, is expressed through goodness, righteousness, and truth. Living in the light also requires separation from darkness, having no fellowship with unfruitful works, and instead exposing them through righteous living. (Ephesians 5:8, KJV)

Reflection

Following the Source of Life

Following Jesus provides a path away from confusion and spiritual darkness. He is the source of life, and our "light of life," representing both eternal life and the spiritual vitality that is strengthened through fellowship with our Lord Jesus Christ. (John 8:12, KJV)

Practical Guidance through the Word

God's Word provides both immediate and long-term direction. A "lamp unto my feet" refers to guidance for the next step, requiring complete faith in God. A "light unto my path" reveals the broader direction and purpose for one's life. (Psalm 119:105, KJV)

A Call for Obedience

Walking in the light is both a personal choice and a collective duty for believers. We are instructed to live according to God's word, reflecting His truth in both private and public life. (Isaiah 2:5, KJV)

Suggested Reading

Specific KJV Passages for Chapter Four:

John 8:12

"Then spake Jesus again unto them, saying, I am the light of the world: he that followeth me shall not walk in darkness, but shall have the light of life."

Psalm 119:105

"Thy word is a lamp unto my feet, and a light unto my path."

Isaiah 2:5

"O house of Jacob, come ye, and let us walk in the light of the Lord."

John 3:21

"But he that doeth truth cometh to the light, that his deeds may be made manifest, that they are wrought in God."

Prayer

Heavenly Father,

Lead me to walk in the light of Your wisdom.

Give me the courage to live openly and faithfully before You.

Let my life be guided by truth and integrity.

In Jesus' name, I pray.

Amen.

Chapter Five

Practicing Integrity Daily

Practicing Integrity Daily

Integrity develops gradually through daily discipline. It is formed in consistent, intentional choices: admitting mistakes rather than hiding them, telling the truth even when it is uncomfortable, and doing what is right even when no one is watching. Faithfulness in even the smallest moments shapes character.

Every choice either strengthens character or weakens it. Each decision becomes part of the foundation upon which a person's life is built. The lasting impact of a righteous life extends beyond the individual. A commitment to integrity can become a legacy, bringing blessings not only in the present but also to future generations.

Proverbs 20:7 (KJV) reads:
"The just man walketh in his integrity:
his children are blessed after him."

Practical integrity is an internal moral compass, guiding daily decisions, treating others with fairness and justice, extending compassion, and living in daily submission to God. Integrity is a multigenerational blessing that shapes and secures a family's future.

Reflection

Practicing Integrity Daily in Scripture

Seeking accountability from those who value honesty and moral courage is a personal commitment to a life of integrity. Daily integrity connects present actions to a lasting legacy of blessings. Scripture teaches that integrity brings stability, security, divine favor, and trust.

Proverbs 10:9 (KJV) states:
"He that walketh uprightly walketh surely:
but he that perverteth his ways shall be known."

Daily Action ("Walketh")
Walking implies a continuous, daily lifestyle rather than a single event. Integrity is not occasional; it is practiced consistently in everyday decisions.

Security and Peace ("Walketh Surely")
Living uprightly provides a firm foundation, producing confidence, stability, and peace of mind.

Accountability ("Shall Be Known")
Dishonesty and crooked paths will inevitably be exposed. This truth encourages consistent and transparent behavior.

Suggested Reading

Honesty and Divine Favor

Truthfulness is not only a social virtue; it reflects a life that pleases God. Scripture teaches that God detests dishonesty but delights in those who act with truth and integrity. (Proverbs 12:22, KJV)

Protection and Preservation

God preserves those who walk uprightly, guarding those who trust in Him. (Psalm 25:21, KJV)

Guidance

Integrity acts as an internal moral compass, guiding daily decisions, while dishonesty leads to confusion and ruin. (Proverbs 11:3, KJV)

Stability

Consistent, honest living removes the fear of exposure and creates a life grounded in trust protected by God. (Proverbs 10:9, KJV)

Lasting Legacy

Integrity is not only personal; it is generational. A multigenerational blessing that shapes a family's future. (Proverbs 20:7, KJV)

Faithfulness in Small Matters

Integrity is developed through daily responsibilities, not only in significant moments or crises. (Luke 16:10, KJV)

Guard Your Heart and Speech

Scripture calls for guarding one's thoughts and controlling speech, avoiding deceit and falsehood. (Proverbs 4:23; Psalm 34:13, KJV)

Choose Honesty Over Gain

God condemns dishonest practices and calls for fairness in all dealings. (Jeremiah 22:13; Proverbs 11:1, KJV)

Keeping Your Word

Integrity requires consistency in speech. A simple "yes" should mean yes, reflecting accountability and truthfulness. (Matthew 5:37, KJV)

Practical Daily Application

Integrity is expressed through just and fair treatment of others, compassion, and a life lived in submission to God. (Micah 6:8, KJV)

Specific KJV Passages for Chapter Five

Colossians 3:23

"And whatsoever ye do, do it heartily, as to the Lord, and not unto men;"

Micah 6:8

"He hath shewed thee, O man, what is good; and what doth the LORD require of thee, but to do justly, and to love mercy, and to walk humbly with thy God?"

James 1:22

"But be ye doers of the word, and not hearers only, deceiving your own selves."

Proverbs 12:22

"Lying lips are abomination to the LORD: but they that deal truly are his delight."

Proverbs 4:23

"Keep thy heart with all diligence; for out of it are the issues of life."

Psalm 26:11

"But as for me, I will walk in mine integrity: redeem me, and be merciful unto me"

Psalm 34:13

"Keep thy tongue from evil, and thy lips from speaking guile."

Jeremiah 22:13

"Woe unto him that buildeth his house by unrighteousness, and his chambers by wrong; that useth his neighbour's service without wages, and giveth him not for his work;"

Matthew 5:37

"But let your communication be, Yea, yea; Nay, nay: for whatsoever is more than these cometh of evil."

Proverbs 11:1

"A false balance is abomination to the LORD: but a just weight is his delight."

Prayer

Heavenly Father,

I ask for Your strength to walk uprightly.

Search my heart and align my desires with Your will.

Help me to live in such a way that my integrity, in private and in public, brings glory to You.

May my actions remain faithful to Your Word.

In the mighty name of Jesus, I pray.

Amen.

Chapter Six

Redemption and Grace

Redemption and Grace

Grace is the source of redemption, while truth is the revelation of our need for it. Redemption is not produced by truth alone; it is granted through grace. Truth exposes. Grace restores. Redemption forgives.

Biblical teaching offers repentance, confession, and the assurance of God's forgiveness. The Bible outlines a journey from guilt to justification. Confession leads to cleansing, while faith in Jesus Christ removes condemnation, transforming the heart through grace.

God's light exists to restore; it does not only reveal wrongdoing, it makes restoration possible.

Ephesians 1:7 (KJV) says:
*"In whom we have redemption through his blood,
the forgiveness of sins, according to the riches of his grace;"*

Repentance opens the door to transformation. Confession breaks the power of secrecy. Truth allows healing to begin. Grace rebuilds what deception has destroyed.

Regardless of the sin one commits, integrity remains a path to redemption. Truth reveals. Grace restores. Redemption comes through the blood of Jesus Christ.

Reflection

The Cost and Source of Redemption

Ephesians 1:7 (KJV) states:

"In whom we have redemption through his blood, the forgiveness of sins, according to the riches of his grace;"

The cost of redemption is the blood of Jesus Christ, and it is given freely by grace. The source of redemption is the "riches of his grace," which reveals that His grace is abundant and not sparingly given.

Theological Foundation: Integrity, Redemption, and Grace

Redemption is both the source and the process by which humanity is restored by God. It is given freely by His grace, not earned by human effort. To be made right with God is a gift, made possible through redemption and sustained by grace.

Redemption is the act of rescue, grace is the unmerited gift that makes it possible, and integrity is the lived result of a transformed life. Through faith, a restored relationship with God calls for a life of moral consistency.

Ultimately, redemption is the act of God buying back humanity from the bondage of sin, paid for by the precious blood of our Lord Jesus Christ. (Romans 3:24, KJV)

Unmerited Favor and Power: God's Grace

Grace is the unmerited gift and favor from God, given to enable people to respond to His call. It is the source of salvation, not human merit.

Grace is both sustaining and active. Sustaining grace, often referred to as sanctifying or habitual grace, is the ongoing work of God that establishes and preserves a believer's spiritual life. Active grace, sometimes called actual grace, is the moment-by-moment prompting and strength that enables a person to respond to God and choose what is right. It establishes a continual state of transformation while also prompting moments of obedience and spiritual awareness.

This is not a limited gift, but an expression of abundant love. Grace allows believers to see God's truth and empowers them to live righteously beyond their own ability. (Ephesians 2:8–9; 1 Peter 1:18–19; Titus 2:14, KJV)

Life Integrated by Grace Is Integrity

Integrity, in this context, is the restoration of what has been fractured by corruption. It is the alignment of one's outward life with their inward convictions as a redeemed child of God.

This restoration is not merely moral behavior, but the result of becoming a "new creation" through the "Grace of God."

Integrity produces a life that is not ashamed to be fully seen, shaped by the indwelling presence of our Lord Jesus Christ. As a result of grace, integrity becomes sustainable.

Those who are believers in Christ do not take redemption for granted, but live in response to it. (2 Corinthians 5:17, KJV)

Application: Redemption a Costly Rescue

Redemption secures the believer. Grace transforms. Integrity becomes the visible fruit of such a transformation.

This foundation motivates believers to live faithfully, restoring integrity in their relationships, vocations, responsibilities, and God's created order.

Redemption extends beyond the soul to the full renewal of life. It addresses the brokenness caused by sin, including fear, shame, conflict, and separation from God. The goal is not only spiritual rescue, but complete restoration.

The ultimate restoration is fulfilled when the redeemed are fully restored, enjoying unhindered communion with God and his creations. (Romans 8:23, KJV)

Suggested Reading

Specific KJV Passages for Chapter Six

Psalm 32:5

"I acknowledged my sin unto thee, and mine iniquity have I not hid. I said, I will confess my transgressions unto the LORD; and thou forgavest the iniquity of my sin. Selah."

1 John 1:9

"If we confess our sins, he is faithful and just to forgive us our sins, and to cleanse us from all unrighteousness."

Isaiah 1:18

"Come now, and let us reason together, saith the Lord: though your sins be as scarlet, they shall be as white as snow; though they be red like crimson, they shall be as wool"

Romans 8:1

"There is therefore now no condemnation to them which are in Christ Jesus, who walk not after the flesh, but after the Spirit"

1 Peter 1:18-19

"Forasmuch as ye know that ye were not redeemed with corruptible things, as silver and gold, from your vain conversation received by tradition from your fathers; But with the precious blood of Christ, as of a lamb without blemish and without spot"

Romans 3:24

"Being justiied freely by his grace through the redemption that is in Christ Jesus:"

Titus 2:14

"Who gave himself for us, that he might redeem us from all iniquity, and purify unto himself a peculiar people, zealous of good works"

2 Corinthians 5:17

"Therefore if any man be in Christ, he is a new creature: old things are passed away; behold, all things are become new."

Romans 8:23

"And not only they, but ourselves also, which have the firstfruits of the Spirit, even we ourselves groan within ourselves, waiting for the adoption, to wit, the redemption of our body"

Romans 3:24

"Being justiied freely by his grace through the redemption that is in Christ Jesus:"

Titus 2:14

"Who gave himself for us, that he might redeem us from all iniquity, and purify unto himself a peculiar people, zealous of good works"

2 Corinthians 5:17

"Therefore if any man be in Christ, he is a new creature: old things are passed away; behold, all things are become new."

Romans 8:23

"And not only they, but ourselves also, which have the firstfruits of the Spirit, even we ourselves groan within ourselves, waiting for the adoption, to wit, the redemption of our body"

1 Peter 1:18-19

"Forasmuch as ye know that ye were not redeemed with corruptible things, as silver and gold, from your vain conversation received by tradition from your fathers; But with the precious blood of Christ, as of a lamb without blemish and without spot"

Prayer

Heavenly Father,

I praise You for Your grace which restores me.

Grant me the strength to align my daily life with Your will, guiding me with integrity so that my work may reflect Your light.

In the name of Jesus, I pray

Amen.

Conclusion

My Walk with God

Conclusion
My Walk with God

For me, I had to distinguish what it truly means to be a practicing Christian. Through that process, I came to understand that attending church is a form of fellowship, a place to worship and collectively express love for our Lord and Savior, Jesus Christ. However, I found that prioritizing a personal relationship with God over and above religious practices is where my faith was solidified.

Reading the Bible and attending church from an early age established a foundation for my walk with God. I have lived an imperfect life, yet I continue to be transformed through a grace-based lifestyle, believing that salvation is a gift from God that cannot be earned through good works. This understanding was not immediate, but it led me to become an ordained minister later in life.

Even as I write this, I am experiencing several significant hardships in my own life. Yet I am filled with gratitude, calm, and a sense of peace because of my unwavering faith in our Lord Jesus Christ and His Word. When I cry, it is not from desperation, fear, or self-pity, but from overwhelming gratitude, knowing He is my protector, my provider, and that I will never be forsaken. The Lord is my shepherd, and I shall not want.

I have experienced enough to be certain that God may allow life to be difficult, but never without providing the grace to endure it.

This is why I accept the responsibility of knowing that I am not perfect, yet I am called to live according to God's Word. To me, integrity is not simply honesty; it is undivided loyalty to God.

Proverbs 3:5–6 (KJV) states:

"Trust in the Lord with all thine heart;
and lean not unto thine own understanding.
In all thy ways acknowledge him, and he shall direct thy paths."

ACKNOWLEDGMENTS

I extend my gratitude to those who have supported, encouraged, and contributed to the development of this work. Your presence and influence is sincerely appreciated.

A special thanks to Ms. Elizabeth J. Rory for reading early drafts and providing invaluable feedback. Your insight and support are deeply appreciated.

Dearest Mrs. Catherine Jones, thank you for modeling a life centered on our Lord and Savior, Jesus Christ and for your lifelong support. Your influence is the bedrock of my life.

ABOUT THE AUTHOR

Shawntel D. Carey is an author, publisher, public servant, and ordained minister committed to creating work grounded in integrity, clarity, and purpose. She has dedicated her work to translating complex principles into practical guidance for everyday life.

Through her writing, Shawntel presents timeless principles in a clear and accessible way, drawing from Scripture, personal reflection, and practical experience. Her work invites readers to examine the quiet places of life where character is formed, and where alignment, authenticity, and consistency shape the course of one's life.

This book is part of her continued effort to provide clear, principled guidance rooted in faith and lived experience.

STAY CONNECTED

We'd love to hear from you.

Email: sdccompasspublishingllc@gmail.com

For updates, new releases, and merchandise:
- **LinkedIn:** SDC Compass Publishing LLC
- **Instagram:** @SDCCompassPublishing
- **Facebook:** SDC Compass Publishing

Share and tag us: **#LessoninIntegrity**

SDC Compass Publishing LLC

Purpose-Driven Publishing, Community Focused.